I0440879

Lower Your Expectations!

An unflinching look at the near future

By David Sadtler

Contents

1 – Introduction

My other piece of advice, Copperfield, said Mr. Micawber, you know. Annual income twenty pounds, annual expenditure nineteen nineteen and six, result happiness. Annual income twenty pounds, annual expenditure twenty pounds ought and six, result misery. The blossom is blighted, the leaf is withered, the god of day goes down upon the dreary scene, and, in short, you are forever floored. As I am! - CHARLES DICKENS, David Copperfield

Britain is a great place to live. The countryside is matchless, its colourful history is everywhere in evidence, and the cultural heritage a reminder of past glories. There has been a continuous negotiation between the country's top management and its people as to what each expects of the other since Anglo-Saxon times. Those with power, wealth, and privilege have managed, with intermittent skirmishes, to keep the people happy enough to allow the political system to evolve at an acceptably sensible pace.

This has been no mean accomplishment. There are only two large population countries on earth that have had the same system of government for longer than since the time of World War II. They are the United Kingdom and the United States of America. All the others fell apart at some point. That's quite an endorsement.

Accountability of government officials is impressive and a lesson to most other countries. Institutions such as Prime Minister's questions provide a very visible challenge to government action and policy, often quite dramatically. The Prime Minister is forced to defend performance on the big issues of the day. Public inquiries like the Chilcot investigation of the Iraq War assess government performance and probity. Politicians are regularly subject to intrusive and irreverent interviews by journalists like Jeremy Paxman and John Humphrys. Corruption seems to be largely confined to silly expense claims by members of Parliament and the BBC hiding the fact that it often employs very badly behaved people. Compare that to the extravagant self-dealing in most Continental countries and in the European bureaucracy in Brussels.

The problem

That's the good news. The other side is that we are headed for tough times and must make some changes to accommodate them.

The rich nations of the West have been living beyond their means for quite some time. This includes Britain. There is nothing new in fiscal irresponsibility. The problem now is that the numbers are so big that it will take a long time to dig ourselves out of and it will be very painful.

The debate between those who argue for stimulus versus austerity is useful and important but ultimately a sideshow. Whatever course of action is pursued, country by country, the result will be the same – a long and painful road to recovery, coupled with a dramatic reduction in the profligacy of the state.

The truth is that it will be a long time before there is any growth of consequence in the UK economy or in that of any other Western country. America under the Obama administration is still experiencing modest growth but only at the expense of huge deficit spending and a lack of fiscal discipline. It is only a question of time before the bond rating services call a halt to this behaviour. All governments are gradually facing up to the necessity to cut costs. That means that any growth in the economy will have to come from business and consumers, not from public spending. Businesses are reluctant to invest because of diminished demand for their products from consumers and other businesses, and consumers themselves are suffering real declines in wages and thus do not have extra money for non-essential expenditures. Most are actually spending less. If extreme, this is called depression. At present it is merely on and off recession. But forget growth anytime soon.

But consumers are still heavily indebted just like their government. Some 18% of UK households classify[1] their debt as being "a heavy burden". Total financial liabilities by individuals has increased from £86 to £95 billion in just two years. People are getting deeper into debt in response to the squeeze resulting from rising prices and level income (see Chapter 2). This debt is a major obstacle to economic recovery. Under pressure, consumers are actually trying to pay down ("de-leveraging") their debts, but what they see as the necessities of life are making this difficult.

In the meantime, there will be conflict between those who feel cheated and those protecting existing interests.

Results

Since families, nations, towns, counties and states are mostly living beyond their means, many have no hope of fulfilling all of their future financial obligations. Eventually the crunch comes. It is happening here and there throughout the world. Here are some examples.

- We all know about **Greece**. This is a country managed by dishonest people, many of whom don't even pay their own taxes. The state kept paying ever greater public sector salaries until it was clear to its bondholding creditors that the money borrowed to do this could never be repaid. The crunch came with a vengeance. It has been terrible. Unemployment is at 25% and unemployment for the youth of

---

[1] According to the Office for National Statistics (ONS)

Greece is now at about 60%. Wages are back down to 1986 levels and pensions have been cut. This all happened because of the cheap borrowing enabled by the euro, which in turn relied on the financial strength of countries like Germany. Investors in Greek bonds were confident that they would be bailed out and were perfectly willing to finance what was clearly not a viable economy. In the event, all private sector bondholders have taken big losses. That lesson will not be lost on the investment community as it looks at comparable situations around the world.

- The town of Stockton California is a similar story. Having lived beyond its means for many years, matters came to a head in the recent recession. The city declared bankruptcy and a huge fight is now underway between bondholders and defenders of its pension obligations. Both will clearly have to take big losses. Stockton is the biggest US city thus far to declare bankruptcy but it will not be the last. As one of the highest crime cities in America, much of the debate in Stockton centres on restoring dismissed police officers and finding a way to finance that.

- The case of Argentina and its default on debt is particularly instructive and harrowing. After years of economic mismanagement, as well as the Falklands war, Argentina in the 1980s and 1990s went through financial chaos with periodic bouts of inflation, currency changes, and political turmoil. It eventually turned to the International Monetary Fund for support. Loans from the IMF and from the USA required further bouts of austerity at a time of great unemployment. Eventually more severe measures were undertaken, including restricted access to bank accounts. Street protests began and grew in intensity. In 2001, the IMF refused to advance the next tranche of loans since the required cuts had not been implemented. At this stage, Argentine debt was yielding 42% above US Treasury levels of interest, clearly an unsustainable position. At that point Argentina defaulted on $123 billion, the largest ever such event. After a subsequent very painful period of austerity, Argentine cash reserves gradually built up and the IMF debt was paid off. But international lenders both public and private will think very carefully before ever lending substantial sums to this government again.

Britain is heading this way as well. By any kind of honest accounting, its future obligations, especially with respect to state pensions (see Chapter 7) cannot be met. The auditors would refuse to certify that the nation's finances are sustainable were Britain a private corporation. Yet we continue to pretend that we will get out of the mess relatively unscathed. The rating agencies, compromised everywhere, will continue to rate the debt reasonably until forced to admit the truth.

There are however fundamental problems of the economy quite apart from the staggering level of government and private debt. Exports are in decline both in manufactured goods and in services. Even after the decline in value of sterling in the last five years performance has continued to decline. The only reason it is not worse is because of growing export performance in raw materials – minerals (oil and gas) and food. In some respects we are beginning to resemble a third world country.

Let us now examine where the expectations are the most likely to result in disappointment.

Blessed is he who has found his work; let him ask no other blessedness. - Thomas Carlyle

Wages in the non-professional sector of the economy, which is the largest sector, are not going up and will not go up in the foreseeable future. Not only is this the effect of austerity and cut budgets, but global competition. World wage rates are converging and fewer and fewer products and services can be protected against foreign competition. Even bypass operations are now being performed, quite adequately, in Mumbai.

Wages in the Euro countries are rising significantly more slowly than inflation. In other words, in real terms they are declining. This is partially the result of high levels of unemployment which lessens the bargaining power of workers with their employers. Employers are simply able to offer less. In Britain, wages are now at the same level as in 2003. Real wages actually dropped by 3% between 2010 and 2012. They continue to do so.

Another more fundamental force is at work here. World wage rates are converging. As developing countries, especially China, are increasingly able to produce anything we can in Britain, jobs are exported to these countries. Even though Chinese workers are demanding greater salaries, they are still at levels some 10 to 20% of those paid in Britain. In such a climate and in such a global marketplace, there is little likelihood that wage costs can be allowed to increase in any significant way in the near future. In America, a country which has traditionally paid its workers more than elsewhere, there has been no real increase in average wage levels for thirty years.

Recent studies have also demonstrated that newly arrived non-EU migrants, to whom we give jobs on six month contracts, are driving down wages. Civil rights campaigners deny this but it is obvious to everyone else. You have only to see the large caravan camps next to harvestable crops, where no English is spoken. If Brits were willing to do the work at the offered wage, they would be hired. The owners wouldn't need to undertake the cost of the caravans.

Wages are a particularly sensitive and even contentious political issue and politicians often fan the flames of any lingering resentment. The term "fat cats" illustrates public and journalistic dislike of highly placed individuals who are seen to make too much money. It has always been thus in Britain but in the current strained circumstances, wages levels in society take on new emotive significance. The notion of disparity and inequity is constantly raised. At present Parliament is expecting to raise its salaries by a significant amount, an initiative opposed by other politicians, many of whom are themselves rich and not in need of an extra few thousand pounds. It's an unseemly debate and story.

But whatever is going on at these higher levels, the fact is that any expectation that wage rates and the attendant standard of living for most people will increase in the near term is bound to result in disappointment. Both the state and the private sector simply lack the capacity and willingness to provide it.

3 - Public sector employment

Asking a town hall to slim down its staff is like asking an alcoholic to blow up a distillery. - from the television series *Yes Minister*

Before the crunch arrived, canny politicians increased public sector employment, often for no economically discernible reason, in order to attract voter allegiance. That is now being wound down. Local councils are cutting back dramatically and more is in prospect. The idea that working for the public sector would be a safe and easy career option is rapidly vanishing.

In the past three years public sector employment in Britain has declined, both in central government and at the local level.

In the Chancellor's 2013 autumn statement, as part of his strategy to tackle Britain's fiscal problems, he announced that automatic pay raises for public sector workers are no longer guaranteed. Most people not in public service might well say "I should think not", but it was still a blow to that portion of the workforce. It is getting tougher and tougher.

The next thing will be pensions. The total UK liability for public sector pensions (see Chapter 7) is now some £1.2 trillion. It is unfunded (i.e., it is paid out of current tax receipts). Economists are generally in agreement that it cannot continue as it stands. That conclusion, when translated into policy by some terrified politician, will be revolutionary.

In reality, the future for public sector workers is clouded in three respects.

- First, we will have to get along with fewer people in these jobs. Some of those presently employed will lose their jobs. This is happening now. Local authorities are cutting back staff levels and we are warned that more on the way. Police numbers are in decline, as are the members of the armed services (see Chapter 5).
- Second, wages will moderate. Automatic increases have now been stopped. The seemingly high salaries of local government officials will be under attack. Whether or not they are changed outright, they are unlikely to enjoy the increases of the past. New hires to such positions will expect less.
- Final salary pension funds ("defined benefit") will be phased out and retirement will take place later. We are only now waking up to the realisation that this principle has become simply unaffordable. Large UK companies are among those coming to this conclusion. One estimate has it that every FTSE100 company will have replaced their final salary funds with contributory systems in the next ten years. In such funds the

amount in the pot at the time retirement defines the benefit. What to some people has seemed liked a cosseted existence will become less so.

If you expect to be a graduate or school leaver in the near future, don't count on government service as a secure and attractive career option, at least in the near term.

I intend to live forever, or die trying. - Groucho Marx

Nowhere are our expectations more likely to be met with disappointment than in the provision of healthcare by the National Health Service. Demand for its services continues to increase dramatically at a time when its budget is under pressure and huge cuts in funding are in prospect. It simply won't be able to provide the same levels of care as in the past.

Last year there were an incredible 50% more operations performed in the NHS than a decade earlier. There were 14.9 million hospital admissions versus 11.1 million. And outpatient admissions in 2011 were 88 million, up 3.8 million in just one year. What is going on? Several factors are conspiring to put every greater pressure on the health service.

- Most important is the increasing prevalence of **unhealthy life styles**. If you have any doubt about the implications of an unhealthy lifestyle, consider what a nurse friend told me not long ago. She said that the wards in the hospital in which she works were filled, nearly exclusively, with people who are obese, get no exercise, don't eat properly and who smoke. There is little question that obesity is imposing an increasingly intolerable burden on the National Health Service. Just treating diabetes, a notoriously life-style-related disease, takes about 10% of the total budget.

- **Alcohol abuse**, is an enormous problem for the National Health Service. Weekend binge drinkers get into fights and car crashes and fill emergency rooms across the land. Some 20% of those admitted to hospitals for any reason at all are judged to have a drinking problem. Diseases arising from excessive alcohol consumption are skyrocketing. Liver cirrhosis deaths are up five times in the last thirty-five years, an appalling development. There are huge obstacles to aggressive programs for treating excessive drinking. The drinks industry itself is highly dependent on excessive drinkers. One estimate has it that if all heavy drinkers drank responsibly, industry sales would decline by 40% and presumably bankrupt some of the participants. Governments are nearly always reluctant to penalise companies that employ a lot of people in Britain. Little will be done.

A Parliamentary Select Committee took a long look[2] at this alarming problem. It is the growing scale of the health problems caused by alcohol consumption which makes it a significant public health issue. The latest Government figures, published at the end of May this year show that There were 6,669 deaths directly related to alcohol in 2010, 22% more than in 2001. In 2010/11, there were 198,900 hospital admissions where the primary diagnosis was attributable to alcohol, 40% more than in 2002-03. In addition, overall there were 1,168,300 hospital admissions which were to some degree attributable to alcohol, more than twice as many as in 2002-2003.

Average consumption, incredibly, has risen from an annual 3.5 litres of pure alcohol per head in 1947 to 9.5 now.

- **Health tourism**. There are growing numbers of people from Eastern Europe and from Africa who arrive in the UK solely to receive medical treatment, especially for complex pregnancies, kidney failure, and treatment for HIV infection, all costly treatments. Often such patients refuse to pay for their treatment and are inclined, often with prior prompting, to claim that their treatment constituted an emergency and was thus free at the point of treatment. There is also fraud. People present themselves for such treatment using someone else's NHS number, a scam which is not always successfully detected and dealt with. Some observers have said that the NHS is becoming the world's maternity ward.

Treating renal failure is one of the most costly services offered by the NHS but one performed better than in most other countries. The attractions thus are obvious. If you have kidney disease, come to the UK on a tourist visa and head right for the hospital. The rules are muddy in such situations and are not always followed by individual hospitals. Often women go directly from passport control to the nearest hospital. The flow of such patients has become a flood and Parliament is now addressing the problem and proposing to limit such services and to charge for them.

- **Asylum seekers**. A recent report[3] by Home Office officials indicates that asylum seekers, of whom there are a lot (and we have lost count), are a burden on the NHS. They have a disproportionately higher number of babies and put strain on maternity services. They have higher TB, Hepatitis B and HIV infection rates and are more likely to need treatment for depression. Language problems also cause considerably delay in GP services.

- **Heightened treatment expectations**. With each new drug, scanning technology, surgical procedure, and other scientific advance in clinical medicine, patients

---

[2] Health Committee - Third Report, Government's Alcohol Strategy, 10 July 2012 (http://www.publications.parliament.uk/pa/cm201213/cmselect/cmhealth/132/13205.htm#note6).

[3] http://bit.ly/167CgKa

demand improved treatment for their illnesses. Each one tends to cost more – there are very few exceptions – as manufacturers and holders of proprietary rights seek to recoup their research investment by aggressive pricing. It is a never-ending cycle. Scanning technology is a case in point. Not many years ago we had only xray. Now we have CT scans, MRI imaging and PET (positron emission tomography) scanning. An xray machine can be bought for about £10k and the cost of xrays in the UK from private sources starts at about £35. CT scans are ten times that amount, MRI scans slightly more and PET scans are from £1k up – sometimes many times that. A PET scanner costs about £4m to buy and set up and £1m per year to operate. It is a miraculous technology. PET scanner are used to asses cancers and are thus a very desirable treatment option. People want MRI and PET scans.

As the founder of the NHS put it, 'We shall never have all we need. Expectations will always exceed capacity. The service must always be changing, growing and improving - it must always appear inadequate.' [4]

- **The ageing population**. Both men and women live an average of 10 years longer than they did before the creation of the NHS in 1948. Predictions for the coming decades envisage more such growth in the older segments of the population. One has it that in the next twenty years the number of people in the UK over 65 will increase by over 50%. This is serious. The cost of providing health care to someone over 85 is three times that of someone between 65 and 85.

The option of simply giving the NHS a lot more money each year is increasingly an unviable one. We are in a new area of limited funding capability – far worse than at any time in recent history. On the contrary major funding cutbacks appear to be in the cards especially in the managerial bureaucracy. Eventually it is likely to reach "front line" services, despite promises to the contrary from political leaders.

If you expect the NHS to deliver timely and effective health care for any and all of your ailments and physiological shortcomings, you are in for disappointment. Be prepared for more rationing. Non-life critical but expensive services like in vitro fertilisation are bound to be curtailed if not terminated. Smokers and the obese will be increasingly refused surgery until they change life styles. That is happening now. I know several large and overweight men who have been refused orthopaedic surgery. Liver transplants for alcoholics who are still drinking will be refused. There will be tough crackdowns on health tourism. Waiting lists will get longer and those who can do so will solve the problem by paying for private care – either individually or through their insurance companies. And – perhaps most controversially – patients will begin to pay for routine events like GP visits. Prescription

---

[4] Aneurin Bevan speaking to a Royal College of Nursing conference in 1950.

charges will rise dramatically. Expectations for treatment by the NHS will clearly need to be lowered. A lot.

5 - Military strength

I have a scheme for stopping war. It's this - no nation is allowed to enter a war till they have paid for the last one. - Will Rogers

Britain has perhaps the most illustrious and heralded military history of any nation in the world. Famous encounters like Crecy, Agincourt, and the Battle of Britain are the stuff of legend and the basis for many a film and novel. But its capability to wage war, at least of the "conventional" sort, is now being called into question.

The British Navy – at one time the world's largest and best and the underwriter of imperial expansion and control - has been undergoing a gradual phasing out in recent decades. At the time of the Silver Jubilee in 1978, the Navy had sixty-nine destroyers and frigates. Now it has nineteen. There were 76,000 serving men compared to 34,000 now. The RAF has one quarter as many aircraft now as it had then. The Army too has been undergoing cuts, reduced now to a total of five brigades. Even so, it is still the second-largest military force in the European Union and it has the fourth largest defence budget in the world after the United States, China, and Russia. Britain can no longer afford this level of expenditure.

The problem is that most of this fighting capability, diminished as it has become in recent years, is less and less relevant to the security needs of the nation. The traditionalist mentality of the armed forces and those who defend their interests was illustrated in a marvellous account[5] by Simon Jenkins of a defence review during the Blair government. He was a lay member of the review committee and was told that it was to be a no holds barred discussion with everything on the table . He was then told that the Trident nuclear program and its submarines, the Typhoon fighter jet, and the plans for three more aircraft carriers were not up for discussion. These three items of course represented the largest items in the defence procurement budget. The restricted discussion reflected the realities of defence industry employment and the Blair government not wanting to be seen to be soft on defence.

Expectations for Britain's military fighting force will have to be more modest. Spending is certain to be increasingly under pressure and the traditional composition of traditional weaponry is on the way out.

---

[5] *Does Britain really need the military?* , Simon Jenkins, The Guardian, Friday 5 November 2010

6 - Law and order

The lack of money is the root of all evil. - Mark Twain

Data show greatly decreasing crime in recent years. All major categories of crime except drug offenses are falling rapidly. Murder and other violent crimes are falling faster than in any other country in Europe. Officials attribute much of the improvement to the greatly increased use of CCTV and DNA profiling. Those who oppose these "intrusions" as violations of their civil liberties are simply misguided. Some may even have the criminals' interests at heart.

But that could change as the economic pressures mount. It is happening elsewhere – for both economic and political reasons.

We seem to have entered an era of massive protest. People are taking to the streets everywhere. The Arab Spring was dramatic and involved widespread public order problems in Tunisia, Egypt, Libya, Syria, Bahrain, and Iraq. As I write, Egypt is virtually in civil war. When people really feel the pinch, they take to the streets.

Protests against austerity measures in indebted Euro-economies are also becoming more strident. Wages in Greece are now at 1986 levels and public sector pensions have been reduced by some 30%. That is why there has been widespread rioting in Greece. It is not helped by the widespread knowledge that top managers and public officials don't pay their taxes even though they have been assessed. These protests will continue, perhaps indefinitely, unless there is a military coup as in Egypt.

Similarly, in Spain there have been widespread protests. As a consequence of the severe belt tightening, Spain's unemployment currently stands at 27% and youth unemployment at over 50%. For many, this is intolerable. Street protests have been growing in the past year.

The anger and unrest reflect not only resentment against the better off but the growing realisation that the old are better off than the young. Not only have the older generation left the young with intractable macroeconomic problems and the prospect of little growth in income and employment, but in most Western countries the retired sector of the population is living better than its youth. It seems likely that young people can no longer automatically assume that their future will be more prosperous than that which their parents experienced. This is something new and it is increasingly apparent and a source of growing resentment.

It is often a seemingly minor event that triggers trouble. In Turkey, people resented the grab of a public park for commercial property development, presumably for the benefit of well connected wealthy people. In Brazil it was about the excessive cost of World Cup preparation. In Bulgaria , people are fed up with government cronyism and corruption. Different issues but the common thread is determined resistance in the street.

Government authorities at times seem powerless to stop such unrest. The so-called social media, especially Twitter and Facebook, are capable of spreading ideas both for protest and to report injustices instantly across countries. Everyone with a smartphone can spread ideas and rumours and even upload photos and videos of riot scenes as they happen to the internet for all the world to see. That is something that even authoritarian regimes cannot really do anything about. Even in China, where the central government is aggressive in trying to control the internet, they appear powerless. There are said to be thousands of riots every single year in China. It appears to be getting worse. We seem to be in a new era. As the truth dawns on the people in the lower social echelons in debt ridden countries, it is likely to get worse. Even Britain will have its share of difficulty and the police will have trouble coping.

In Britain the police struggle to prevent crime and to respond aggressively to citizens fears of it. Civil libertarians constantly seek to restrict surveillance, the treatment of criminals and even the procedures involved in arrest and trial. The police themselves seem to resist any form of reform or procedural change. They also demonstrate inordinately high levels of sickness and other reasons to take benefits in lieu of work.

Should widespread unrest develop as a consequence of the financial pressures on us, the law enforcement authorities, having themselves endured cutbacks, could disappoint in their ability to control it.

7 – Pensions

In the name of Hypocrites, doctors have invented the most exquisite form of torture ever known to man: survival. - Edward Everett Hale

Private sector pensions have been decimated in recent years in a variety of ways. Pension funds are required to minimise speculative investment and focus their investment allocation on fixed interest securities, which means bonds. Unfortunately the yields on bonds are at record lows and providing adequate returns increasingly difficult. Furthermore management charges are thought to be excessive. According to the FSA, existing pension pots have been reduced by some 30% through charges. Abusive practices abound and the regulatory authorities have been only marginally effective in dealing with them.

Further, the state's treatment of private pension pots has been destructive. Gordon Brown famously eliminated the tax benefit from dividends for pension funds, a huge blow to the size of pensions. It was a £5 billion tax grab, one of a number of such measures by the government of the day. Pension pots still suffer from it.

At the same time, vast numbers of people have no savings and no investments, especially those at the bottom of the income ladder. Only 34% of people are thought to have any kind of savings for their retirement. Those without are the people who most need it.

But there is a real question about whether the state can continue to fill the gap, as it has in the past. An excellent report[6] on a conference dealing with this issue and describing the views of the Office of National Statistics, helps to clarify the nature and extent of the government's challenge.

The total obligation of the UK government for state pensions is £3.8 trillion[7], all of it unfunded. That means that there is no pot from which this money will come, as there must be for commercial companies. Rather, everything that comes in through pension contributions from wage earners is immediately paid out to pension recipients and if necessary topped up by the government. As the number of people in retirement grow faster than those in work, it is easy to see that this cannot continue at its present rate.

---

[6] http://www.if.org.uk/archives/2031/ons-reveals-full-uk-pension-liabilities
[7] If it's any consolation, the figure for France is 6.7 trillion euros (£5.7 trillion). Germany is even higher.

One organisation undertook to investigate the sustainability of pensions in the UK[8]. Since this is a mathematically complicated subject and one replete with political bias, they sensibly recruited fifty well-known economists to give their views. You may be sceptical about how much economists really understand about the world around them, but at least they have the time and tools to undertake the kind of analysis necessary to form an intelligent view. It's a lot more than you can expect of any politician. The results were predictably depressing. Over half said that it was certain that public sector pensions would not be paid in full. These are the pensions that are expected by people now working in the public sector, not at some undefined moment in the future. They were also in agreement that the state's impossible liability for state pension would gradually be reduced through a variety of mechanisms. They will be means tested, as is now the case in Australia, retirement age will be increased, the indexation to reflect inflation will be weakened, and worker contributions will be increased. A huge but necessary series of changes.

The government pensions minister recently announced that an automatic link is soon to be established between pension age and longevity. In other words, as people live longer and longer, the age at which they receive their pensions will automatically increase to reflect it.

The European authorities are having a constructive effect in this area. They are now requiring all states to provide a supplementary table in their annual accounts to assess their overall pension liabilities – this is the 2008 System of National Accounts (SNA2008) and the 2010 European System of Accounts (ESA2010) . Britain has been the first to comply with this requirement. I wonder how long we will have to wait for compliance from the Mediterranean countries. Can you imagine what the pension liability statement for Greece will look like?

Those who expect the state to do an adequate job of looking after them in their old age, especially if they are so improvident as not to have saved anything, are in for crushing disappointment. The state simply cannot afford to continue present levels of payment, let along make them more generous. They will also have to work a lot longer. The days of early retirement, except for the financially very successful, are fast disappearing.

Reduce your expectations and spend accordingly.

---

[8] David Kingman, *Can the UK Afford To Pay For Pensions? 50 expert economists give their view*, March 2013, Intergenerational Foundadtion

I described the euro as a burning building with no exits and so it has proved for some of the countries in it. - William Hague

The Common Market: We went into it to screw the French by splitting them off from the Germans. The French went in to protect their inefficient farmers from commercial competition. The Germans went in to purge themselves of genocide and apply for readmission to the human race. - From the television series, Yes Minister

The European cooperative venture now known as the EU did a good job with its original purpose, that of preventing further wars in Europe – at least in the Western part of Europe. Specifically it was designed to prevent Germany from trying again. It was even useful and constructive in breaking down trade barriers – the formation of the so-called single market.

Then it decided to grow further and extend its influence into every sphere of economic and cultural activity among its growing membership. A cynic might even conclude that much of this activity was initiated to further the interests of a burgeoning bureaucracy in Brussels. In any case, Brussels has brought us a series of disasters.

Most notable was the introduction of **the euro**, an idea opposed by many economists but rushed through by politicians who were either ignorant of economic realities or chose to ignore them for their own political ends. I need not rehash what went wrong but suffice it to say that it enabled countries less economically capable and less honestly governed to borrow money very cheaply, thus enabling themselves to enter the twilight mess in which they now find themselves. It has been an unmitigated disaster. And despite the optimistic pronouncements by the President of the European Commission as well as the President of France, it is still with us and will be indefinitely. It is a major cause of the awful economic problems with which we are now trying to deal.

Second it brought us the **common agricultural policy** a funding programme greatly benefiting the French which for many years has consumed most of the EU budget. It keeps food prices in Europe high, shuts out competition from Third World producers, and burdens European taxpayers. Attempts are now being made to reduce it. Those attempts are being fiercely opposed by the obvious vested interests. It is a monster pure and simple.

Rules for running businesses and our lives are imposed on individual countries and are often inappropriate and deeply resented. The thirty-five hour week is a classic example, probably the worst economic initiative in recent memory, started at a time when labour productivity is sluggish but needs to become more efficient. It does the opposite, but it is a favourite of optimistic ideologues and politicians, as well as that of trade unions seeking to cushion the lives of their members as their bargaining power in other ways diminishes.

Finally, there is the question of **human rights**. A constant barrage of decisions from the European court on how people must be treated in each country. It prevents Britain from being able to deport the worst kind of criminals and terrorists. It is an aspect of Europe that is simply not wanted here in Britain by anyone except the most left-leaning ideologues.

In recent years there has been increasing public agitation about Britain's membership in the European Union. Much of it arises because of what is seen to be as interference in Britain's ability to govern itself. If European authorities inhibit Britain's ability to attack its financial condition and to deal with the problems and frustrations noted above, the nation will become ever more alienated from it. It seems likely that that will happen.

The real crime of Europe has been to raise expectations across the board. Countries have been deluded into thinking that they can afford to provide a lifestyle for their citizens vastly in excess of the strength of their economies. And the rights of workers have been protected while the competitive posture of the region is in long-term decline. The authorities have a lot to answer for and, in many respects, they are responsible for the crisis in expectation. Those who view European institutions as a benign force in our lives are in for disappointment. Either its influence will be dramatically reduced or Britain will withdraw.

9 - Heartening developments

Common sense in an uncommon degree is what the world calls wisdom. -
Samuel Taylor Coleridge

As of mid-2013 the Coalition is addressing the debt problem, unlike its predecessor, and people are reducing household debt. They are both doing this with the full realisation that lower expenditures represent a downshift in consumption spending. People are indeed starting to get the message about expectations. There are a number of signs that we are headed in the right direction.

1. Cuts are being accepted – so far. Debate in Parliament and comments in the press, even the populist tabloids, accept the need for reduced state spending. It is not denied. The argument is about what to cut and how to balance the books.
2. My NHS still works responsively. If you believed every newspaper report you would think that NHS treatment was poor and even unavailable. That's not my experience. On the relatively few occasions I have had to avail myself of NHS services, I have been treated courteously, effectively and in a timely way. But it is still up against near impossible pressures, to which it will be forced to respond.
3. Tax evaders are being pursued. At long last individuals and companies who evade or avoid tax are being pursued. The government of the day has always protected its rich friends and party contributors, but the financial pressures of today make that no longer an option. Many have become an embarrassment. They also pursuing tax havens like the Isle of Man, the Channel Islands, and Grand Cayman, all otherwise inconsequential places that live off of tax reduction schemes. The whistle is at long last being blown.
4. Military objectives and resource allocation are being redirected without much fuss. Last week our local regiment passed through the streets of our town, to the applause of onlookers as they retrench and head back to a vastly reduced future elsewhere. It was a poignant moment but a reminder of how conventional soldiering by brave men is increasingly unaffordable and headed for replacement by cyber warfare geeks in front of computer screens. It's a reality and we are facing it.

Britain is a sensible, well governed place. Sometimes it gets things wrong, but the mistakes are eventually addressed and put right. That is what is happening now.

Life is not a matter of holding good cards, but of playing a poor hand well. - Robert Louis Stevenson

It is clear that Britain is going through a tough transitional period. But for individual citizens, the pain can be acceptable as long as expectations are reduced and moderation introduced. There are some specific things you can do.

1. Think twice before embarking on a career in public service or the military. Obviously there are rewarding and challenging jobs to be had in these sectors of the economy. But don't count on a fat pension after a modest time in service.
2. Get fit to lessen your dependence on health care delivery. Stop smoking, eat sensibly, get exercise, and moderate your drinking. Stopping smoking is mandatory unless you want to die of lung cancer or contract emphysema and drag an oxygen tank around behind you. Both are horrible diseases. You don't want to get them. Getting to the right weight is just as important. If you are serious about losing weight, you really have to do three things. Most importantly, you have to eat the right things. Weight loss is hopeless without this. Second, you must moderate how much you eat. Third, you must get exercise. For more on this see my book, *Fifty Great Weight loss Tips* (http://amzn.to/10vFcUA). Moderate drinking is the other vital component of a healthy life style. Too much and you can encounter liver failure and a variety of cancers.
3. Learn to live on a lot less. You need enough to eat and you need adequate shelter and protection from excessive cold in the winter. Your health care is free. Everything else is discretionary and to varying degrees can be dispensed with. You don't need a plasma TV. Make your own list of what you don't need and then act on it. Otherwise you could even become a bankrupt or a homeless outcast.
4. Save. Unless you want to live in penury in your old age, you had best provide for it. The state will surely fall short. Find someone who is good at math and you can find out how much you have to save.

In sum, downscale your expectations and downshift your lifestyle.

Author

David Sadtler is a career writer, teacher, and management consultant specialising in corporate strategy and finance. He has published a number of books and many articles on these subjects. Although still counselling on various investment projects, he has increasingly focused his concern and attention on social issues. In a number of books, he addresses obesity, since it is becoming the leading public health problem worldwide. Another describes the problems of the Catholic Church in the context of an agenda for the new Pope. This book addresses another huge problem with social, ethical, and financial implications.

They are all available on Amazon.

He can be contacted at david.sadtler@gmail.com and would welcome your comments.

www.ingramcontent.com/pod-product-compliance
Lightning Source LLC
Chambersburg PA
CBHW071351310526
45790CB00018B/1418